ENDANGERED
DESERT ANIMALS

Dave Taylor

Crabtree Publishing Company

ENDANGERED ANIMALS SERIES
Text and photographs by Dave Taylor

To Anne, who always supported me

Editor-in-chief
Bobbie Kalman

Writing team
Dave Taylor
Bobbie Kalman
Janine Schaub
Dave Schimpky

Editors
Janine Schaub
David Schimpky

Design and computer layout
Antoinette "Cookie" DeBiasi

Cover mechanicals
Rose Campbell

Photograph
page 12-13 by Peter Laurie

Separations and film
EC Graphics Ltd.

Printer
Worzalla Publishing

Published by
Crabtree Publishing Company

350 Fifth Avenue
Suite 3308
New York
N.Y. 10118

360 York Road, RR4
Niagara-on-the-Lake
Ontario, Canada
L0S 1J0

73 Lime Walk
Headington
Oxford OX3 7AD
United Kingdom

Cataloguing in Publication Data
Taylor, Dave, 1948-
    Endangered desert animals

(The endangered animals series)
Includes index.
ISBN 0-86505-534-3 (library bound) ISBN 0-86505-544-0 (pbk.)
Wars and industrial development are some of the dangers faced by desert wildlife.

1. Desert fauna - Juvenile literature. 2. Endangered species - Juvenile literature. 3. Wildlife conservation - Juvenile literature. I. Title. II. Series: Taylor, Dave, 1948- The endangered animals series.

QL116.T39 1993   j591.90954

Contents

Not all deserts look alike. As you can see, some deserts support many plants (top). Other deserts are barren and lifeless rock (left). The desert in the bottom right picture is the sand-dune type desert we usually think of when we hear the word "desert."

The world's deserts

The desert experience

It is July in Death Valley, and your feet feel as if they are being burned right through the soles of your shoes. Without any wind, the desert is absolutely silent. All the animals and insects are lying motionless in their hiding places, trying to escape the scorching heat.

Although you have already had ten glasses of water, you are still thirsty. It is so hot that you pour a little of your drinking water over your head and immediately start to shiver. The moisture on your skin is evaporating so quickly into the dry air that you feel cold. In about a minute, you are completely hot and dry again. You find it hard to believe that you will need a heavy jacket for warmth when the sun goes down. Can you imagine what it would be like to be an animal living in this desert year round?

Deserts defined

Deserts can be found around the world. They cover about one-eighth of the planet's surface. Deserts are not always hot places. Any dry, or **arid**, region is called a desert when it receives less than 10 inches (25.4 centimeters) of precipitation a year.

Rain and snow fall on the desert, but the precipitation is always unreliable. Sometimes the total precipitation for a year can fall during a single storm. At other times, there may be no precipitation for many years. Most or all of the rain and snow that falls in a desert evaporates.

Contrasting landscapes

Not all deserts look like the huge sand dunes shown in the bottom right picture on the opposite page. Desert landscapes vary from a bare patch of rock in the mountains of North America to a huge plain of salt in Ethiopia.

Some deserts have pavement-like surfaces, whereas others are scrub-covered mountain landscapes. A blanket of miniature flowers can carpet the ground of some deserts after a summer storm; other deserts are so dry and lifeless that they resemble the surface of the moon.

Forever changing

Radar images sent to the earth by the space shuttle Columbia in 1981 showed that the Sahara Desert was not always a dry region. Far beneath the dunes lie ancient river valleys! These radar images demonstrate that desert areas do not stay the same.

In some deserts, sands are slowly taking over the nearby semi-desert areas. In other places deserts are getting smaller, or **retreating**. Some scientists believe that the number of deserts on our planet is increasing, and others believe the opposite. Most agree, however, that desert landscapes are forever changing.

What makes deserts dry?

Deserts can be dry for a variety of reasons. Moisture-laden clouds rarely reach deserts that lie far away from oceans. In some dry areas, the air is calm. There are no winds to blow in rain-bearing clouds. Some coastal deserts are formed because winds traveling across cold ocean currents cannot hold enough water to make rain, although they may produce fog.

Other deserts are dry because mountain ranges prevent rain from reaching these areas. Rain-bearing clouds are forced into the cooler air at the tops of the mountains. The cool air causes droplets of rain to form and fall on the mountains.

When the clouds reach the other side of the mountains, there is little, if any, moisture left.

Causing deserts to form

In many parts of the world people are responsible for creating deserts. When people move into arid regions and overuse the land, deserts can form.

When semi-desert lands are cleared for farming, the topsoil often dries up and blows away. Sometimes deserts can result from improper methods of watering crops. Seawater makes soil too salty for plants to grow. Farm animals such as goats and cattle can overgraze dry areas and turn them into deserts in which nothing can survive.

A desert full of life

Most deserts appear barren and lifeless, supporting few plants and animals. The Sonoran Desert, on the other hand, supports a large number of plants and animals because it receives a fair amount of precipitation. Over 100 types of cacti can be found there.

Is it really a desert?

Although the Sonoran Desert has more vegetation than the desert areas that surround it, it is still a desert. For most of the year, the land is dry and the summer temperatures are very hot. Even when it rains, the sandy soil is unable to hold water for very long, and the land is soon dry again.

(opposite) The Sonoran Desert, located in the southwestern United States, appears quite green compared to other deserts.

Rainstorms are rare in the desert. The animals and plants that live there depend on these occasional storms for the moisture that guarantees their survival.

Desert plants

The scattered vegetation found in most desert areas has adapted to harsh conditions. Desert plants must be able to survive extreme temperatures and cope with little water. Without moisture, the ground is so dry that particles of sand cannot bind together to support plant life.

Conserving moisture

To exist in the desert, plants have developed ways of surviving without a reliable source of moisture. Many plants do this by producing seeds each year until they die. The seeds then wait, sometimes for as long as 50 years, for the rain to make the ground wet enough for their roots to sprout.

Collecting water

Other desert plants collect water year after year, using ancient survival strategies. Some have long, tough roots that find water deep below the surface of the earth. Others depend on a wide system of shallow roots to collect surface moisture. Still other desert plants rely on special waxy, leathery, or hairy leaves that help them retain water.

(above) The prickly pear is a type of cactus. Its waxy leaves prevent water from evaporating in the heat. (right) In order to hold moisture, the roots of the saguaro cactus form a shallow mesh up to 90 feet (27 meters) in diameter around the plant. During the rains, these roots gather water and store it in the vertical pleats of the plant. The pleats can expand and hold up to one ton (1016 kilograms) of water! This water is poisonous to animals. (below) The spines of the barrel cactus help protect this plant from being eaten by animals.

(above) This lizard lives in semi-arid desert regions. Its sand-colored body helps it stay cool by reflecting heat away. As a result, this lizard can tolerate very high temperatures but, when it gets hot, it cools down in the shade. (below) The kit fox, which lives in the deserts of the southwestern United States, fights the heat by staying in its cool den during the day. It does its hunting at night.

How desert animals cope

The survival of animals depends on how they have adapted to desert life. The bodies of some desert animals have changed over millions of years to cope with a lack of water and extremes in temperature. The Merriam kangaroo rat, for example, has developed specialized kidneys that process tiny amounts of concentrated urine. This allows the kangaroo rat to conserve water without damaging its body organs.

Overheating

Many desert animals have developed ways of protecting themselves from overheating. Some have big, thin ears that provide a large surface where their blood can be cooled. There are lizards whose sand-colored bodies help them stay cool by reflecting heat away from them. Most large desert animals, such as the bighorn sheep, have thin bodies and slender legs. All these features help desert animals stay cool.

Desert ways

Other animals have also developed ways of protecting themselves from desert conditions. The African gerbil conserves its body moisture by resting during the heat of the day and becoming active in the cool of the night. If it must move around in the daytime, it does so by hopping about quickly on its tiptoes!

Arctic areas can also be desert-like. During winter, when there is a shortage of drinking water, polar bears eat only the blubber of seals. They leave the seal meat behind because too much water is required to digest the protein in meat.

Quietly waiting

Many desert animals are **dormant** during the dry season. Dormant animals lie so still that they seem almost dead. They remain in this state until the desert rains arrive. When there is no rain, many desert animals, such as the Asian gerbil, stop having babies. By not carrying babies, this animal's chances of survival are increased. Some desert birds become ready to breed immediately after a rainfall.

*Rattlesnakes cannot tolerate high temperatures. They avoid the extreme daytime heat in protected shelters called **burrows**.*

Animals in danger

In recent years many desert animals have become endangered due to hunting and the loss of their habitat. The millions of people around the world who make desert lands their home often compete with native species for plant and animal resources.

Terms of endangerment

Worldwide conservation groups use various terms to describe animals in distress. Animals that are **extinct** have not been seen in the wild for over 50 years. Animals referred to as **endangered** are likely to die out if their situation is not improved. **Threatened** animals are endangered in some areas where they live. Animals that are **vulnerable** may soon move into the endangered category if the causes that put them in danger continue to exist. **Rare** animals are species with small populations that may be at risk.

A delicate balance

Desert life can be difficult and sometimes impossible if the delicate balance of water, plants, and wildlife is upset. Once desert lands are overused and all the plants are gone, rain that used to fall may stop entirely. Deserts without rain are unable to support life.

Dromedaries have been domesticated by desert-dwelling people. They are particularly important to **nomads,** *people who constantly move about the desert in search of grazing land. Dromedaries are famous for their ability to go without water but, when these animals get thirsty, they can drink up to 100 liters (26.4 gallons) of water at one time!*

The Bactrian camel

A camel with two humps is called a Bactrian camel. The Bactrian camel is darker, shorter, stockier, and shaggier than the dromedary, its one-humped relative. Only two wild herds of this endangered animal still roam the Gobi Desert. One herd is in China, and the other is in Mongolia. No one knows how many Bactrian camels live in China; only 400 to 500 survive in Mongolia.

Camels sent packing

About 4000 years ago, there were still great numbers of wild Bactrian camels roaming Asia. When people discovered that these camels were excellent desert travelers and pack animals, they domesticated them. As a result, there are few Bactrian camels left in the wild.

Today "tame" Bactrian camels can be found in zoos around the world and trading caravans in Asia. They have bigger feet, humps, bodies, and more hair than their wild relatives.

An ancient species

An ancient species, Bactrian camels are descendants of the camel family that developed in North America 40 to 45 million years ago. Two or three million years ago, all the different types of camels left North America, although no one knows why. Some camels moved to South America where, over time, they evolved into llamas. Others moved to Asia, where they developed into the one-humped and two-humped camels.

Life in the Gobi Desert

In the Gobi Desert the life of a wild Bactrian camel follows a yearly pattern. The temperature in this "cold" desert area ranges from -20°F (-29°C) in winter to over 100°F (38°C) in summer! During the heat of summer Bactrian camels may climb to a cooler altitude of 11,000 feet (3350 meters) or more. They return to the lower, warmer areas in winter.

Loose sand and gravel

Bactrian camels are well suited for walking on the loose sand and gravel of their desert home. Thick eyelashes and nostrils, which can be opened and closed, protect them from blowing sand. Their wide hoofs allow them to walk across deep sand without sinking. Their weight does not rest on the tips of their toes; it is spread out over the padded soles of their hoofs.

Fill 'er up!

Bactrian camels, like other camels, are famous for their ability to go without drinking for long periods of time. Some people claim that these animals can survive without water for up to ten days! During dry periods, camels get the water they need from the plants they eat. When they get a chance to drink at a watering hole, they make the most of the opportunity. A thirsty Bactrian camel can drink almost 30 gallons (114 litres) of water at one time!

Height: 75-91 inches (200-230 centimeters)
Weight: 1000-1450 pounds (450-657 kilograms)
Where it lives: Mongolia and China

Bactrian camels have adapted well to desert life. Their wooly hides protect them from the heat and also slow down sweating, thereby conserving moisture.

The dromedary

The dromedary is a single-humped camel. Scientists estimate that there are about 14 million camels wandering the earth and, of those, nine out of every ten are dromedaries! Six out of every ten dromedaries live in Africa.

The dromedary has been extinct in the wild for about 2000 years, but we do not think of it as extinct because we see it so often in zoos, circuses, and movies.

Beasts of burden

Originally, wild dromedaries were found in the Middle East and North Africa. These camels were taken from their desert homes by people who saw their great potential as domestic animals. They were first domesticated about 4000 B.C. and were eventually exported to most countries that had deserts. Dromedaries are ideally suited for desert transportation. They are also a source of milk, meat, and leather.

Dromedaries groan when they are loaded and unloaded, often bite their handlers, and can be quite smelly. Although these animals are not the most pleasant animals to deal with, they have been used as beasts of burden for centuries!

The helpful hump

The dromedary can survive long periods without water because of the fat stored in its hump. This fat changes to water to meet the camel's body needs. A 90-pound (41-kilogram) hump can give the camel about 45 quarts (42.5 liters) of water. Dromedaries can live without water ten times as long as humans and four times as long as donkeys.

Cool when it counts

Dromedaries conserve their body's water reserve by perspiring only at very high temperatures. These camels also stay cool by allowing their body temperature to vary. A dromedary's body temperature can vary by as much as 11°F (6°C). A person whose temperature varied that much would be very sick! When the weather gets hot, the dromedary's temperature rises to keep it from sweating. This adjustment helps the dromedary save body moisture.

Where dromedaries run wild!

Wild dromedaries have been extinct for so long that it is impossible to know what kind of lives they led. Some scientists are interested in studying a few **feral** herds found in Australia, Africa, and in small numbers in Asia. Feral is the term used to describe domestic animals that have started living in the wild.

Height: (to top of hump) 75-91 inches (190-230 centimeters)
Weight: 1000-1450 pounds (450-650 kilograms)
Where it lives: Southwest Asia, north Africa, Australia

The dromedary belongs to the same family that also includes antelopes, cattle, bison, sheep, and goats.

The Gila monster

Gila monsters are classified as vulnerable because much of their habitat in the southwestern United States and Mexico has been taken over by people.

These lizards are active at night and remain hidden during the day. People who live in the Gila monster's home range hardly ever see these reptiles.

A Gila monster "dugout"

During hot days in the desert, Gila monsters live in holes under the ground. The temperature below the desert surface remains almost the same year round, no matter how hot or cold the weather. Gilas can dig their own holes but often use holes dug by other desert dwellers.

Poison glands

The Gila monster is one of only two types of poisonous lizards in the world. The other is the beaded lizard of Mexico, which is a close relative. Both lizards have poison glands located on the lower jaw. Snakes have their deadly glands on the upper jaws, above their needle-like fangs.

Rarely fatal to humans

A Gila monster cannot inject its poison the way a snake can. Its venom flows along the grooves in the teeth of its lower jaw. This reptile must chew into its prey, or the poison will not reach the victim's bloodstream. Although painful, Gila monster bites are rarely fatal to human beings.

Smelling their prey

At night or during cool days, the Gila emerges from its hole ready to hunt. It uses its tongue to scoop air into its mouth. On the roof of its mouth is the sensitive **Jacobson's organ**. This organ uses the sense of smell to locate prey.

The Gila monster eats rodents and birds, as well as the eggs of birds and reptiles. Once attacked, these small animals die quickly from the Gila monster's poisonous bite. The lizard then swallows its prey whole!

Slow movers

Gila monsters are not very fast-moving creatures, but most of their prey are! This means that sometimes these reptiles must wait for days between meals. Fortunately, Gila monsters are capable of going without food for long periods of time by living off the fat stored in their tails.

Although Gila monsters have adapted to living without water for long periods, they are surprisingly good swimmers! Flash floods from unexpected rainstorms are not a problem for these lizards!

Length: 18-24 inches (46-61 centimeters)
Weight: 2 pounds (.9 kilograms)
Where it lives: Southwestern United States to western Mexico, Guatemala

---

Gila monsters can live up to 20 years in captivity. They have only a few enemies in the wild—coyotes, hawks, and people.

Gila monsters have scales that look like shiny beads. The scales help them retain moisture.

The scimitar-horned oryx

The oryx is a large African antelope that grazes in semi-desert areas. The word "scimitar" is used to describe this animal's gracefully curving horns, which resemble a Persian sword by the same name. The scimitar-horned oryx uses its horns to chase weaker members of its species away from choice grazing areas.

The oryx was once found around the fringes of the Sahara Desert in north Africa. Just 100 years ago, herds numbering close to 1000 animals were found, although groups of 20 to 40 were more common. By 1850 the oryx was extinct in Egypt and, by the middle of the twentieth century, it had disappeared from the northern part of its range. There were still small numbers left in the southern portion of its habitat, but today fewer than 10,000 of these oryxes remain on the edge of the Sahara desert.

A casualty of wars

During the desert fighting in the two world wars, the number of oryxes was greatly reduced. These animals were killed for food or used for target practice by bored soldiers. After the wars, many more oryxes were killed by desert nomads who had acquired modern weapons from the armed soldiers.

Domestic pressure

The scimitar-horned oryx survived the pressures of war in small numbers, but it faced an even bigger problem afterwards. As the population of Africa increased, so did the herds of cattle and goats raised by farmers. These animals required huge amounts of food and quickly devoured the oryx's food supplies in the semi-desert areas. Herds of goats did the most damage. They ate all the ground cover as well as the leaves of trees. Goats can climb and strip a tree's leaves, leaving nothing for the native wildlife!

Government protection

The governments of two African countries, Chad and Tunisia, have been working to save the oryx. In 1986, a zoo-bred herd was introduced back into the wild in Tunisia. In Chad an oryx reserve has been set up to allow the number of these wild antelopes to increase under government protection.

Height: 4 feet (1.2 meters)
Weight: 450 pounds (204 kilograms)
Where it lives: In a narrow strip of the Sahara Desert between Mauritania and the Red Sea

Zoos are playing an important role in saving the scimitar-horned oryx from extinction. Young oryxes born in captivity are being successfully returned to the wild.

The addax

The addax is an antelope that is truly at home in the Sahara Desert of north Africa. It wanders in groups of up to 20 animals, looking for the sparse desert vegetation that is its food.

Thousands of years ago, the addax was taken from its desert home and domesticated by the ancient Egyptians. The Egyptians made the addax carry loads and sacrificed it during religious ceremonies. Desert dwellers depended on this animal for food and leather. It was not surprising that by the early 1900s the addax had died out in Egypt.

Senseless slaughter

During World War II, the armies that fought in the desert used machine guns to kill entire herds of addax. By the end of the war, the addax was almost extinct in the Sahara Desert. By 1970 there were only 1500 left in the country of Chad, where once there had been thousands. By 1990, only twenty years later, there were fewer than 1000 left in all of Africa.

A diet that saves lives

The addax is now protected throughout its entire range. The chances of its survival are good because it is one of the few wild animals in the world that does not eat any of the foods that people or their domestic animals eat. Even if people move into its desert home, the addax will not have to compete with domestic herds for food. The addax may be further protected by its attraction to hostile desert environments. What feels like home to the addax would be unbearable for most people!

Height: 42 inches (106 centimeters)
Length: 6.5 feet (2 meters)
Weight: 275 pounds (125 kilograms)
Where it lives: Mauritania, Mali, Chad, Algeria, Sudan

The addax is well adapted to its harsh desert home. It can go without water for long periods of time, obtaining moisture from the coarse grasses that grow in the desert. Both male and female addax have horns, which help them chase other addax away from food.

Prezwalski's horse

The ancient species of wild horse, called Prezwalski's horse, is virtually extinct in its native Mongolian habitat. Overhunting, combined with the spread of the growing human population, has seriously reduced this horse's number. Although one scientist was recently able to photograph a single stallion, people are still searching for the small Mongolian herd to which this wild horse may belong. Because many domestic horses have interbred with Prezwalski's horses, it is believed that this small herd may contain the only pure wild horses left on the planet!

Rifles spelled doom

For centuries Chinese and Mongolian hunters killed small numbers of Prezwalski's horses for food. In later years, modern rifles enabled hunters to kill many more of these animals. By 1879 Prezwalski's horses were already in danger of becoming extinct.

One big family

In an attempt to save these animals from extinction, 32 Prezwalski's horses were captured. These horses formed the breeding stock that eventually populated the zoos of the world. Scientists were concerned that the offspring from this one herd might become weakened because the parents were too much alike. In 1947 zoo workers looked for other wild horses but were able to capture only one stallion. Today most of the 1000 wild horses born in the world's zoos are descendants of this one horse. Today over 100 zoos raise herds of Prezwalski's horses.

A new life in a cold desert.

If the wild Mongolian herd is ever found, zoos around the world hope to introduce the captive animals back into their native habitat. Scientists hope that once these animals are established, they will live in the Gobi Desert in western Mongolia just as their ancestors did.

Surviving winter

Long ago the warm southern slopes of the mountains and grassy plains of Mongolia were used by Prezwalski's horses as their autumn and winter home. This sunny and sheltered area offered them protection from the snow. In the spring and summer, herds of up to 20 animals moved into the scrub desert to graze on a variety of grasses. Although most adult animals were hardy enough to survive desert conditions, many foals died in the late winter storms of April and May, which are the birthing months of these wild horses.

Height: 4.5 feet (1.4 meters)
Length: 9 feet (2.8 meters)
Weight: 440-660 pounds (200-300 kilograms)
Where it lives: Near the Altai mountains of Mongolia

Fossils show that this small wild horse was once found in North America but became extinct near the end of the last ice age. Prezwalski's horse is the size of a pony and is the only horse to have a stiff, brushlike mane.

Desert bighorn sheep

The desert bighorn sheep is a subspecies of the familiar bighorn sheep seen in North America's Rocky Mountain parks. Although all types of bighorns are endangered, the desert bighorn sheep is the most endangered of all.

Many causes of endangerment

Desert bighorn sheep are now protected in the deserts of Nevada, California, Texas, and Mexico, but they are still killed illegally. Hunters value their horns as hunting trophies. As more and more people move into desert areas, the bighorns are threatened by the loss of their grazing areas and watering holes. Domestic donkeys, called **burros**, that live in the wild compete with these sheep for grass. A lack of food is also responsible for the decline in the number of bighorns. Diseases from domestic animals have helped reduce the herds as well.

Large ranges

Good grass is hard to find in desert areas. As a result, the bighorn sheep must graze a large range in order to find enough food to eat. Being scattered over such a vast area has affected the breeding behavior of these animals. Male bighorns seek mates from July to November, making this the longest mating season of any wild sheep. They require a long mating season to locate the females.

Living in the heat

Researchers studying the bighorn marvel at this animal's ability to withstand heat.

It is not uncommon to see sheep grazing under the heat of the desert sun when the temperature soars to 110°F (43°C). This sheep's ability to go without water is also extraordinary!

Moisture from plants

Unlike its northern relative, the desert bighorn does not need to drink very often to meet its water requirements. It gets the moisture it needs from the plants it eats. This bighorn does, however, rely on some permanent watering holes during the hottest summer days.

A water fight

People living in the desert cities of Las Vegas, Nevada, and Palm Springs, California have taken over most of the bighorn's sources of water. Fortunately, in recent years people in these cities realized the damage they did to the sheep and began to provide sanctuaries with access to watering holes. Now the best places to see these rare sheep are near these two cities.

Length: Male: 63-72 inches (160-182 centimeters) Female: 51-63 inches (129-160 centimeters)
Weight: 200 pounds (91 kilograms)
Where it lives: Southwestern United States and Mexico

Like all sheep, bighorns are excellent climbers and like to rest on steep slopes. From there they can see their enemies approaching. These include coyotes, cougars and humans.

(above) The coat of the jaguarundi can be a reddish chestnut color or a dark gray. (left) In humid, jungle areas, the ocelot's fur is orange. In the desert, however, its coat is gray. (below) The bobcat is most active at night, seeking the small animals it eats. This animal prefers to hunt alone. Its favorite meal is rabbit.

Desert cats

Endangered cats

The ocelot, jaguarundi, and bobcat are among the rarest desert cats in North America. All are listed on the endangered species list. None is strictly a desert animal, although all three can be found in the deserts of the American southwest. The ocelot is more common in the jungles of central and South America, the jaguarundi in the dense forest thickets of Mexico, and the bobcat in the forests of North America.

The ocelot

At one time the ocelot was found across most of the southwestern United States, Mexico, and as far south as Argentina. In the 1960s and 70s it was considered fashionable for women to wear coats made from the fur of this spotted cat. During this fur-coat-fashion period, the ocelot almost disappeared from its range in North America. Thanks to protesters and government legislation, the hunting of ocelots has stopped. Sadly, this magnificent cat has not made much of a comeback in its former range. Its future is in doubt.

Nighttime hunters

Ocelots usually live in pairs and, like most spotted cats, prefer to hunt at night. In the desert they eat animals such as rabbits, rodents, young deer, birds, and reptiles. During the day they curl up in the shade of a hollow log or crevice and sleep.

The jaguarundi

Jaguarundi are found in the southern United States, Central America, and most of South America. Throughout their range their number is declining, and they are almost entirely gone from their desert homes.

Facing many challenges

Jaguarundi became endangered because they lost their desert habitat and were overhunted. Farmers still shoot them because they attack domestic animals.

The jaguarundi has a small head and long slender body, which help it sneak through heavy bush cover. Like the ocelot, the jaguarundi eats small animals.

The threatened bobcat

The bobcat also makes its home in the deserts of North America. It is endangered for several reasons. Its beautiful fur makes it a target for hunters. The bobcat also suffers from habitat loss, as cities and farms spread into wilderness areas.

Length:
Ocelot: 36-60 inches (91-152 centimeters)
Jaguarundi: 21-30 inches (53-76 centimeters)
Bobcat: 28-50 inches (71-127 centimeters)

Weight:
Ocelot: 35 pounds (16 kilograms)
Jaguarundi: 10-20 pounds (4.5-9 kilograms)
Bobcat: 13-68 pounds (6-30 kilograms)

Where they live:
Ocelot and **Jaguarundi:** Arizona to Argentina
Bobcat: Southern Canada to Mexico

Preserving desert habitats

The best way to understand the delicate ecosystem of the desert is to visit a desert. If you cannot take a trip to a real desert, visit a natural-science museum that has a desert display. Once you learn about the great variety of desert life, you will become interested in preserving it.

Animals caught in the battle

Many of the species in this book have become endangered because of war. Recent battles in the Middle East, some of which still continue, threaten wildlife populations in these regions. Until warring desert people solve their differences, human and animal lives will continue to be at risk. Are there any local animals in your community that are caught in the middle of people's disagreements?

Local action

Many semi-desert areas have been turned into deserts by improper farming and water-conservation methods. Find out if farm land near your home is being damaged in similar ways. Are there ways to improve the land? Do you think these methods could also be used in desert areas? Why or why not?

Animal kidnapping?

The dromedary was removed from the wild so it could be used by people. Today it only exists as a domestic animal. If you visit a desert or another wilderness area, never remove any animal from its natural home. Animals have a right to remain in their home just as people do.

The desert in the picture above is called Death Valley.

Glossary

arid Dry; having little rainfall

blubber The layer of fat on some sea mammals

burros Small donkeys that live in the wild

conservation Protection from loss, harm, or waste, especially of natural resources such as wildlife

Death Valley A very hot and dry desert area located in California

domesticate To adapt or tame an animal for human use

dormant Temporarily inactive; sleeping

endanger To threaten with extinction

environment The setting and conditions in which a living being exists

evaporation The change of a liquid into a vapor

extinct Not in existence; not seen in the wild for over 50 years

feral herd A wild or untamed herd of animals that were once domesticated

Gobi Desert Desert located in central Asia, mostly in Mongolia and China

habitat The natural environment of a plant or animal

Jacobson's organ A highly sensitive organ used for locating prey by smell; found on the lower jaw of the Gila monster

llama A South American animal closely related to the camel

Middle East An area that includes parts of southwestern Asia, Turkey, Arabia, and northeastern Africa

nomad A person who wanders from place to place looking for pasture for his or her animals

population The people or animals of an area; the total number of individuals living in a particular area

precipitation Water that falls to earth, including rain, snow, or hail

prey An animal that is hunted by another animal for food

range An area over which an animal roams and finds food

rare Uncommon; in serious danger of becoming extinct

Red Sea The sea between Saudi Arabia and northeastern Africa

reduce To make smaller

reserve Land set aside by the government for a special purpose

resource Something that is made use of for aid or support

Sahara Desert The largest desert in the world; located in northern Africa

scimitar A curved Persian sword

scrub Low trees or bushes

specialized Adapted to a particular environment

species A group of related plants or animals that can produce young together

stallion A male horse

steppe A broad, grassy plain in Europe or Asia

subspecies A group of animals within a species

threatened Describing an animal that is endangered in some parts of its habitat

urine Liquid body waste

vulnerable Capable of becoming endangered

Index

2 3 4 5 6 7 8 9 0 Printed in USA 2 1 0 9 8 7 6 5 4 3

DATE DUE
